I0816925

An Imprint of Pop!
popbooksonline.com

The Eras of Taylor Swift

THE TORTURED POETS DEPARTMENT era

Track List...

1. Fortnight (ft. Post Malone)
2. The Tortured Poets Department
3. My Boy Only Breaks His Favorite Toys
4. Down Bad
5. So Long, London
6. But Daddy I Love Him
7. Fresh Out The Slammer
8. Florida!!! (ft. Florence + The Machine)
9. Guilty as Sin?
10. Who's Afraid of Little Old Me?
11. I Can Fix Him (No Really I Can)
12. loml
13. I Can Do It With a Broken Heart
14. The Smallest Man Who Ever Lived
15. The Alchemy
16. Clara Bow

*track list continued on page 17

by Elizabeth Andrews

This book is filled with videos, puzzles, games, and more! Scan the QR codes* while you read, or visit the website below to make this book pop.

popbooksonline.com/TTPD

abdobooks.com

Published by Pop!, a division of ABDO, PO Box 398166, Minneapolis, Minnesota 55439.

Printed in the United States of America, North Mankato, Minnesota.

082025
012026

Cover Photo: Alexandra Tarasova (BigArtLab); Shutterstock Images

Interior Photos: Getty Images, Guy Corbishley/Alamy Stock Photo; Scott A Garfitt/Invision/AP; Shutterstock Images; Terry Dean/Alamy Stock Photo; Thomas Jackson/Alamy Stock Photo

Editors: Grace Hansen and Anna Schwartz

Series Designer: Laura Graphenteen

Library of Congress Control Number: 2025941229

Publisher's Cataloging-in-Publication Data

Names: Andrews, Elizabeth, author.

Title: The Tortured Poets Department era / by Elizabeth Andrews

Description: Minneapolis, Minnesota : Pop!, 2026 | Series: The eras of Taylor Swift | Includes online resources and index

Identifiers: ISBN 9781098248772 (lib. bdg.) | ISBN 9781098249298 (ebook)

Subjects: LCSH: Swift, Taylor, 1989- --Juvenile literature. | Popular music--Juvenile literature. | Popular (Songs, etc.)--Juvenile literature. | Albums--Juvenile literature. | Concerts--Juvenile literature. | Mass media and music--Juvenile literature.

Classification: DDC 782.42164102--dc23

*Scanning QR codes requires a web-enabled smart device with a QR code reader app and a camera.

TABLE OF CONTENTS

CHAPTER 1
Ruining Her Life 4

CHAPTER 2
Love and Poetry 10

CHAPTER 3
Behind the Lyrics 16

CHAPTER 4
The Show Isn't Over 24

Making Connections. 30
Glossary 31
Index. 32
Online Resources 32

CHAPTER 1

RUINING HER LIFE

In February 2024, Taylor Swift posted a moody, warm-toned, black-and-white photo of herself lying in bed. It featured the words *The Tortured Poets Department* (*TTPD*). The caption read, "All's fair in love and poetry... New album THE TORTURED POETS DEPARTMENT. Out April 19." A new era was beginning!

WATCH A VIDEO HERE!

Meet Taylor

Birthday: December 13, 1989
Star Sign: Sagittarius
Place of Birth: West Reading, PA
Favorite Number: 13
Favorite Color: Purple
Favorite Food: Chicken tenders and a chocolate shake

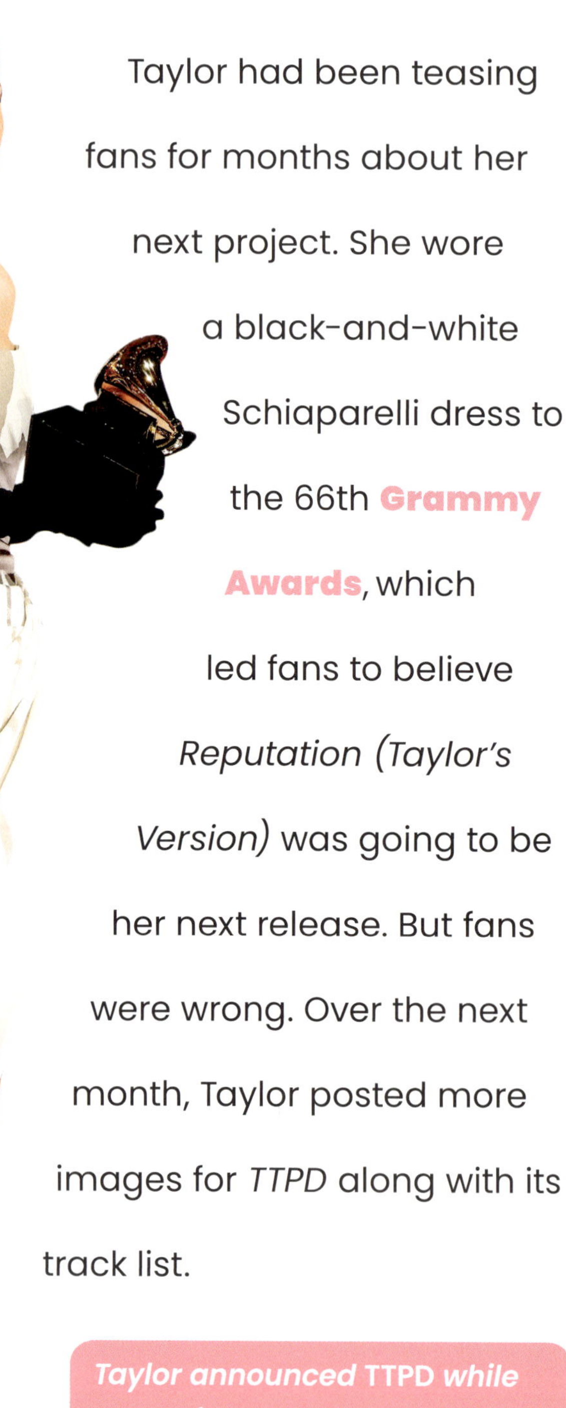

Taylor had been teasing fans for months about her next project. She wore a black-and-white Schiaparelli dress to the 66th **Grammy Awards**, which led fans to believe *Reputation (Taylor's Version)* was going to be her next release. But fans were wrong. Over the next month, Taylor posted more images for *TTPD* along with its track list.

***Taylor announced* TTPD *while accepting the Grammy for Best Pop Vocal Album for* Midnights.**

The first **single** off *TTPD* was not released until the album dropped. She used an Instagram video to take fans from a *Midnights*-themed room through a hall and into The Tortured Poets Department. Posted on the wall of the department office was a calendar with a note about the release date and time for the "Fortnight" music video featuring Post Malone.

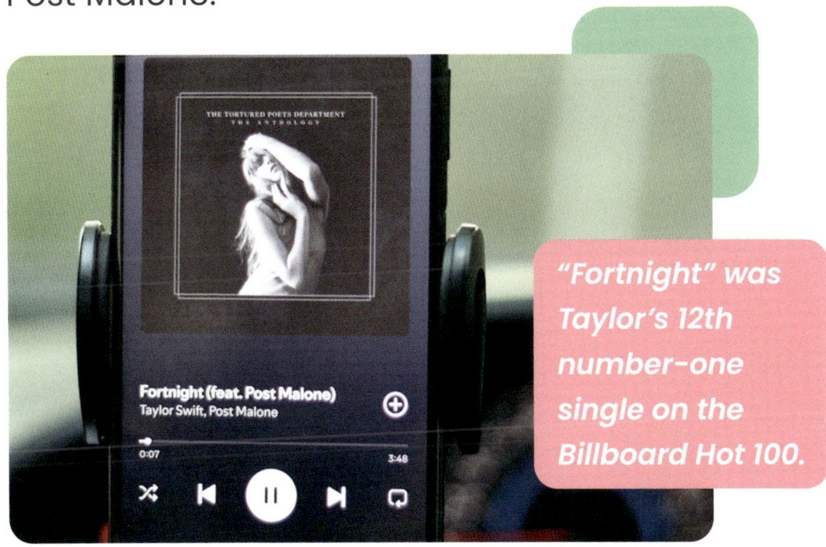

"Fortnight" was Taylor's 12th number-one single on the Billboard Hot 100.

Taylor wrote and directed the music video for "Fortnight." She said everything in the video connects to different parts of the album. It is shot in black and white with old-style dresses and typewriters to match the album's color theme. In a behind-the-scenes video, Taylor shows how she sneaks Easter eggs into the shots while filming.

This is a dress worn by Taylor in the "Fortnight" music video.

Easter Egg

Famous actors Ethan Hawke and Josh Charles have roles in the "Fortnight" music video. They are known for a film called *Dead Poets Society*.

In 2024, Taylor Swift and Post Malone won the MTV Video Music Award for Best Video for "Fortnight."

CHAPTER 2

LOVE AND POETRY

Taylor's 11th **studio** album, *The Tortured Poets Department*, was released at midnight on April 19, 2024. Two hours later, Taylor dropped 15 more songs to make *TTPD: The Anthology*. Taylor explained that The Tortured Poets Department

EXPLORE LINKS HERE!

People used feather quills dipped in ink to write until the mid-1800s.

refers to a government organization that studies the minds of poets. Historically, poets have been misunderstood.

There are four versions of the TTPD album cover.

Snow Graffiti

Easter Egg

Taylor has written about many poets in her music. She specifically loves the Romantic poets from late 18th- and early 19th-century England.

WRITING UTENSILS

Taylor has said her songs are "titled Quill Lyrics, Fountain Pen Lyrics, and Glitter Gel Pen Lyrics." Quill lyrics are from songs that feel old-fashioned. Many songs from *folklore* and *evermore* have these lyrics. Fountain pen lyrics are modern stories with poetic twists. Taylor says most of her songs fall into this category. Glitter gel pen lyrics are happy and carefree. "Bejeweled" and "22" are examples of glitter gel pen songs.

Fountain pens have ink inside that is fed to the writing point as needed.

One of the album's themes is dark **academia**. Before *TTPD* was released, Taylor crafted a life-size display of a poet's study. Fans wandered through and found hints about what the album would bring. There were items like fountain pens and quills on the desk.

Taylor worked with her good friend and producer Jack Antonoff (far right) on TTPD.

Taylor and Joe were together for six years!

Most Swifties assumed *TTPD* would expose Taylor's breakup with Joe Alwyn. However, the album is mostly about Taylor's on-again, off-again love interest, Matty Healy. The album's main storyline is about Taylor feeling intense desire for a new object of love. *TTPD* was a tool Taylor used to process her **scrutinized** public and private life. The album was self-aware, funny, angry, and sad.

Matty is in the band The 1975.

CHAPTER 3

BEHIND THE LYRICS

TTPD: *The Anthology* has 31 songs. Every song has lyrics that make it clear how masterful Taylor is at building stories and emotions. The title track might be based on a group chat Joe Alwyn had with his friend Paul Mescal that they called the "Tortured Man Club."

COMPLETE AN ACTIVITY HERE!

...Track List Continued

17. The Black Dog
18. imgonnagetyouback
19. The Albatross
20. Chloe or Sam or Sophia or Marcus
21. How Did It End?
22. So High School
23. I Hate It Here
24. thank you aIMee
25. I Look in People's Windows
26. The Prophecy
27. Cassandra
28. Peter
29. The Bolter
30. Robin
31. The Manuscript

Matty and Taylor dated publicly for a few weeks in 2023.

In "Down Bad," Taylor sings about how hard it is to go back to normal life after experiencing a brief "cosmic love." Like an alien **abduction**, Taylor wonders if the romance was too crazy for people to believe. This song is likely about Matty. It mentions how Taylor's abductor enjoys stirring up trouble in the public eye. Fans think Matty's poor **reputation** is what led to the couple's breakup.

Taylor wore a sparkly UFO dress to the 2024 MTV VMAs.

The fifth song on Taylor's albums is usually the saddest. "So Long, London" is the fifth song on *TTPD*. Joe is from London. It was a special place for the couple. The song is about trying to keep a relationship from falling apart. It ends with Taylor finally realizing that the effort she is making is not worth it. The relationship makes her too sad and she must let it go.

"I Can Do It With a Broken Heart" is a classic Taylor pop gem. The music builds

The first line of "So Long, London" mentions fairy lights. "Lover" and "Cornelia Street" are love songs about Joe that mention lights to symbolize home.

The breakups with Joe and Matty took place while Taylor was on the Eras Tour.

slowly, preparing for the beat to finally drop. The lyrics share the heavy things Taylor was going through during the Eras Tour. She was heartbroken and working harder than ever. But she showed up every night for her fans with a smile on her face.

Taylor and Travis show each other support by going to one another's games and performances.

While much of *TTPD* is about boys Taylor is ready to leave in her past, there is one song that rings of hope for a new man. "So High School" is written about a romance full of giggles, small moments, and an **adolescent** view on love. The line "you know how to ball" suggests this song is about Taylor's new boyfriend, football player Travis Kelce.

Easter Egg

In the lyric video for "So High School" Taylor highlights her and Travis's initials in the line "Cheeks pink in the twinkling lights."

CHAPTER 4

THE SHOW ISN'T OVER

Taylor dropped *TTPD* in the midst of the Eras Tour. Fans were curious how she would add more music to her already 3-hour-long show. Starting on May 9, 2024, in Paris, France, Taylor performed

LEARN MORE HERE!

Taylor used showgirl fans in her TTPD *set. They were an Easter egg for her next album,* The Life of a Showgirl*!*

TTPD after the *1989* set. To make space for it, she combined the *folklore* and *evermore* sets into one.

Taylor's TTPD *dress is covered with lyrics from the album's songs.*

TTPD's section of the tour had white set pieces including a bed similar to the one used in the "Fortnight" music video. Taylor had three costumes, featuring a white gown with a fluffy skirt covered in writing. When she sang "Down Bad," a

The light from the UFO made it seem like Taylor was in the middle of an alien abduction.

UFO filled the screen and beamed her around the stage. The set ended with a costume change for "I Can Do It With a Broken Heart." Travis Kelce once joined the dancers for this song.

Fans wrote the names of the boys they considered to be the smallest men to ever live.

TTPD was a writing project first and an album second for Taylor. She used it to process everything she learned and lost through her past relationships. When she shared the album with the world, she also shared a poem to explain what the album meant to her.

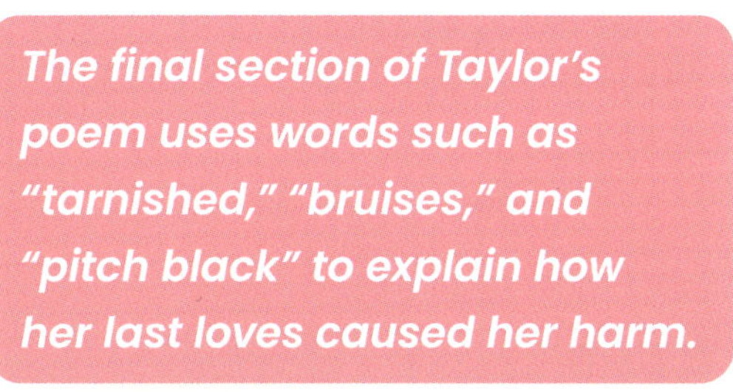

The final section of Taylor's poem uses words such as "tarnished," "bruises," and "pitch black" to explain how her last loves caused her harm.

...And so I enter into evidence
My tarnished coat of arms
My muses acquired like bruises
My talismans and charms
The tick, tick, tick of love bombs
My veins of pitch black ink

All's fair in love and poetry
Sincerely,
The Chairman
of The Tortured Poets Department

muses: people who inspire an artist to create art.

talismans: objects carried to protect from evil and bring good luck.

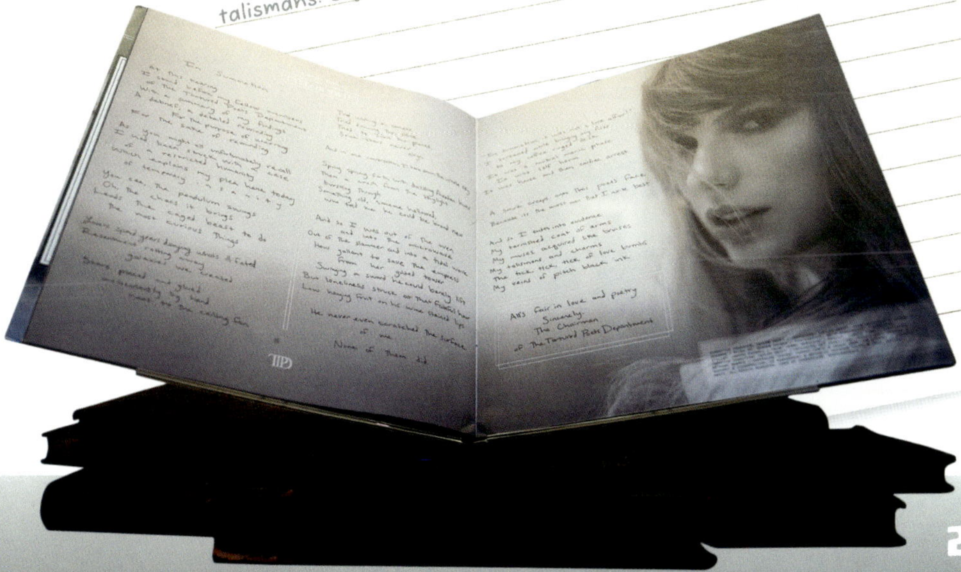

MAKING CONNECTIONS

TEXT-TO-SELF

What is your favorite song from *The Tortured Poets Department* Era? Why is it your favorite?

TEXT-TO-TEXT

Have you read books about any other music artists? How are they similar to or different from Taylor Swift?

TEXT-TO-WORLD

As a reader, why do you think so many people around the world connect with Taylor Swift and her music? Write a few sentences to explain your answer.

GLOSSARY

abduction — the act of being taken by force. An abductor is the one who commits the act.

academia — the life, community, or world of teachers, schools, and education.

adolescent — feeling or acting like a young person who is growing into adulthood.

Grammy Awards — an event that recognizes and awards remarkable works in music throughout the year.

reputation — the level of respect given to someone by the public.

scrutinize — to look at closely and carefully, with attention to detail.

single — a song that is released as a stand-alone from the album.

studio — a place where recordings are made.

INDEX

Alwyn, Joe, 14, 16, 20
Anthology, The, 10, 16
awards, 6

"Down Bad," 18, 26

Eras Tour, 21, 24
evermore, 25

folklore, 25
"Fortnight," 7, 8, 26

Healy, Matty, 14, 18–19

"I Can Do It With a Broken Heart," 20, 27

Kelce, Travis, 23, 27

Malone, Post, 7
Mescal, Paul, 16
Midnights, 7

poets, 11, 13

"So High School," 23
"So Long, London," 20

Tortured Poets Department, The, 4, 6–7, 10, 12, 14, 16, 20, 23–26, 28

writing utensils, 12–13

DiscoverRoo!
ONLINE RESOURCES

This book is filled with videos, puzzles, games, and more! Scan the QR codes* while you read, or visit the website below to make this book pop.

popbooksonline.com/TTPD

*Scanning QR codes requires a web-enabled smart device with a QR code reader app and a camera.